**Time,
our most precious commodity.**

The Persian Alphabet

We want to simplify your Persian learning journey as it is such a unique & enigmatic language. There are 32 official Persian letters. The letters change form depending on their position in a word or when they appear separate from other letters. For example, the letter ghayn غ has four ways of being written depending on where it appears in any given word:

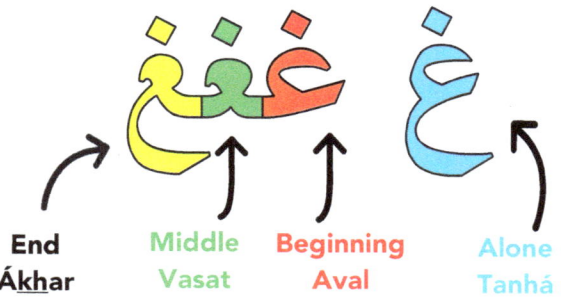

End	Middle	Beginning	Alone
Ákhar	Vasat	Aval	Tanhá

It is important to note that Persian books are read from right to left (←). There are 7 separate/stand-alone letters that do not connect in the same way to adjacent letters (these will be depicted in blue). They are:

Stand alone
Tanhá vámístan

The short vowels a, e & o are usually omitted in literature and are depicted by markings above & below letters (ـَـ). They are not allocated a letter name, unlike their long vowel counterparts á: alef, í: ye & ú: váv (و ى آ).

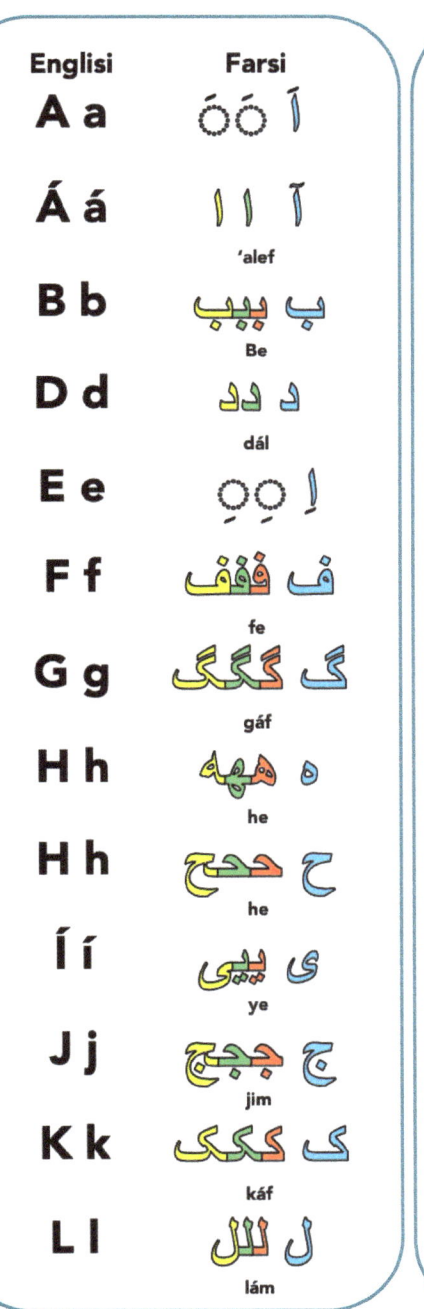
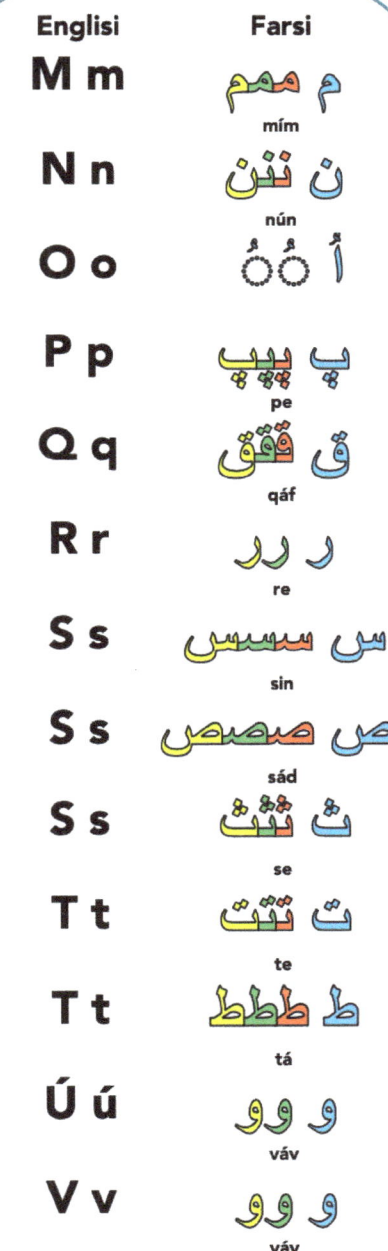
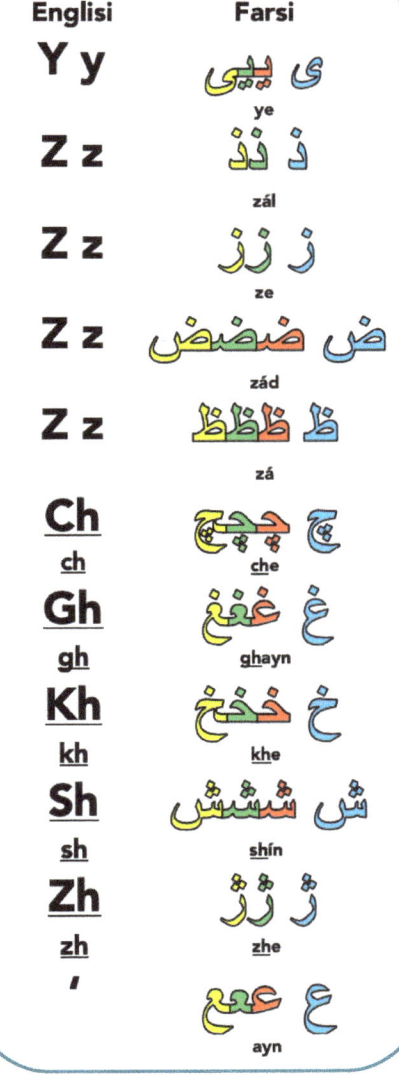

Letter Guide©

Pronunciation Guide©

Persian	English	Pronunciation
اَ	a	ant
آ	á	arm
ب	b	bat
د	d	dog
اِ	e	end
ف	f	fun
گ	g	go
ه	h	hat
ح	h	hat
ی	í	meet
ج	j	jet
ک	k	key
ل	l	love
م	m	me
ن	n	nap
اُ	o	on
پ	p	pat
ق	q/gh*	merci
ر	r	run
س	s	sun
ص	s	sun
ث	s	sun

Persian	English	Pronunciation
ت	t	top
ط	t	top
و	ú	moon
و	v	van
ی	y	yes
ذ	z	zoo
ز	z	zoo
ض	z	zoo
ظ	z	zoo
چ	ch	chair
غ	gh*	merci
خ	kh*	bach
ش	sh	share
ژ	zh	pleasure
ع	'	uh-oh†

*	: guttural sound from back of throat
†	: glottal stop, breathing pause
ّ	: Indicates a double letter
ً	: Indicates the letter n sound
لا	: Indicates combination of letter l & á (lá)
ای	: Indicates the long í sound (ee in meet)
ایـ	: Indicates the long í sound (ee in meet)
(...)	: Indicates colloquial use

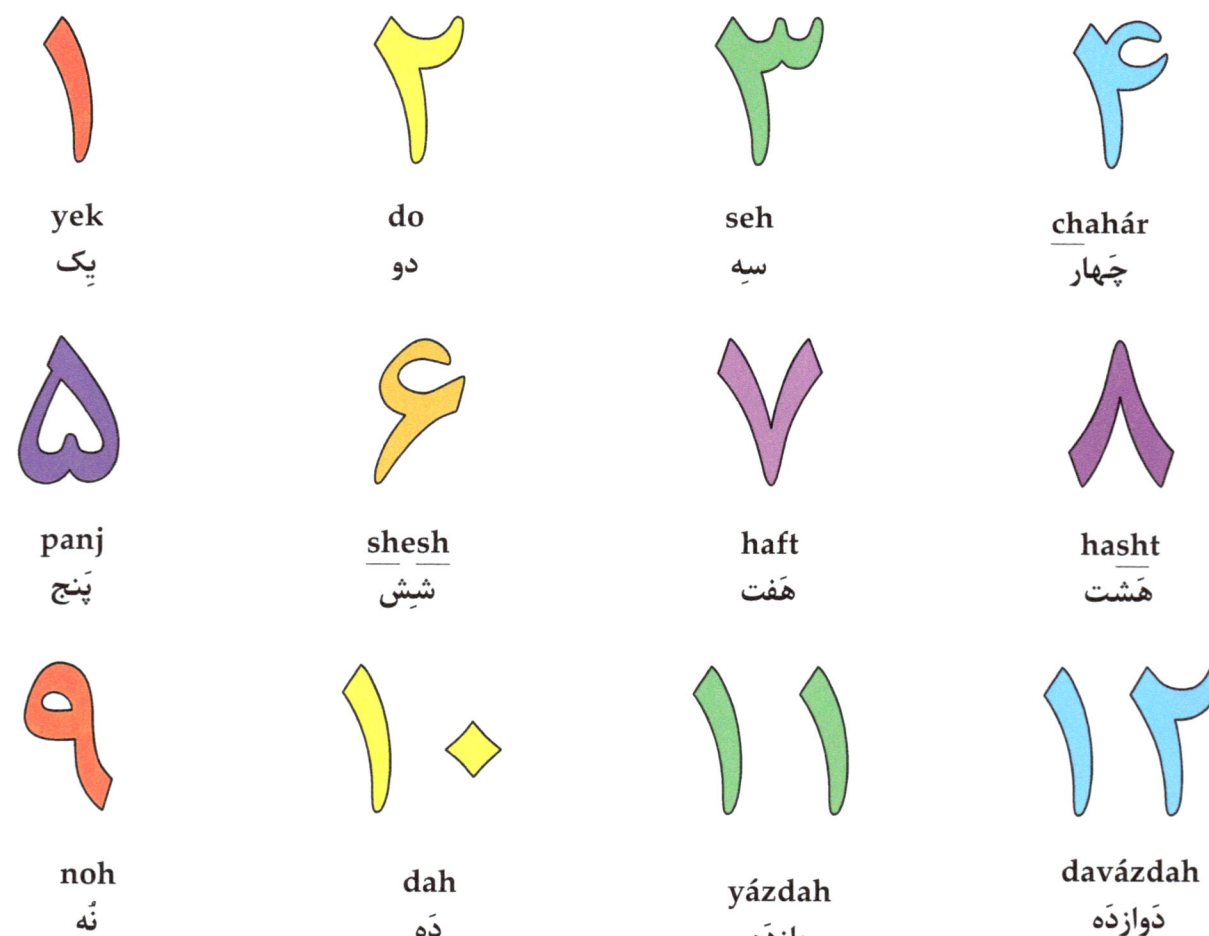

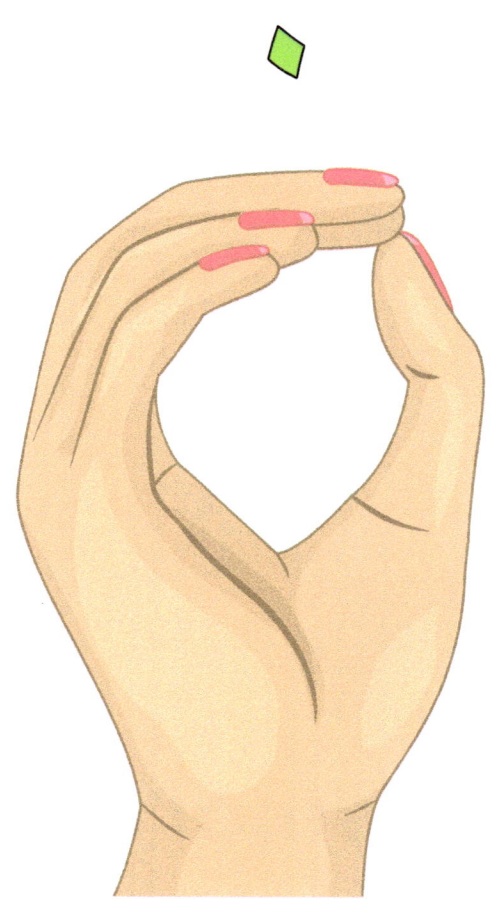

zero

sefr

صِفر

one

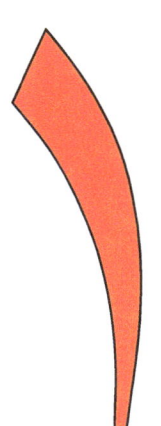

yek

یِک

١ ٢

two

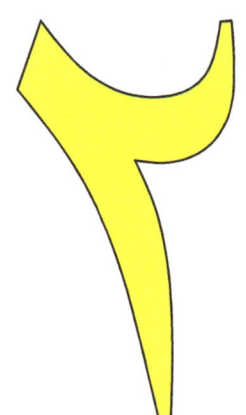

do

دو

١ ٢ ٣

three

seh

سِه

۱ ۲ ۳ ۴

four

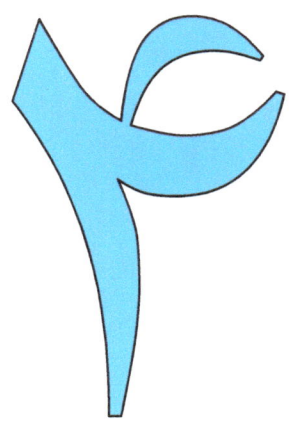

chahár

چَهار

á: as (a) in arm

۱ ۲ ۳ ۴ ۵

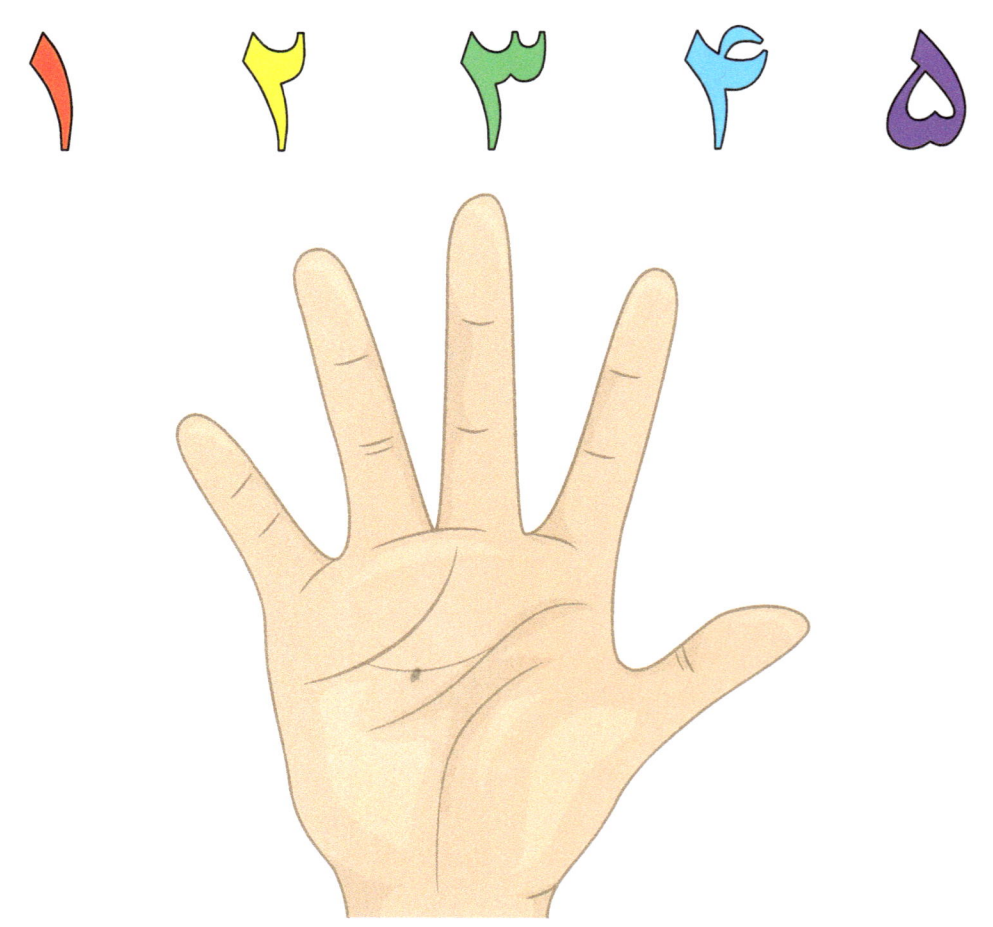

five

panj

پَنْج

۱ ۲ ۳ ۴ ۵ ۶

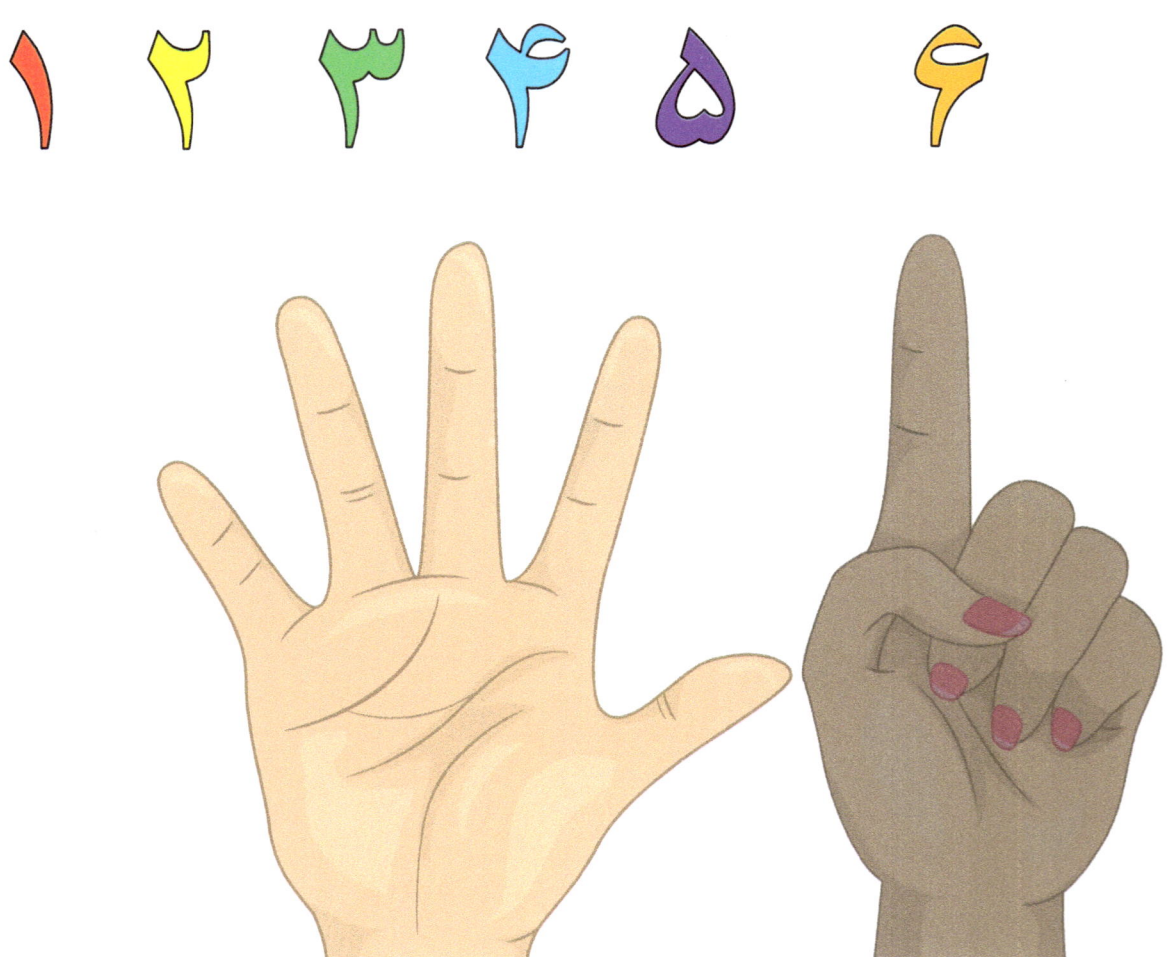

six

s<u>h</u>es<u>h</u>

شِش

۱ ۲ ۳ ۴ ۵ ۶ ۷

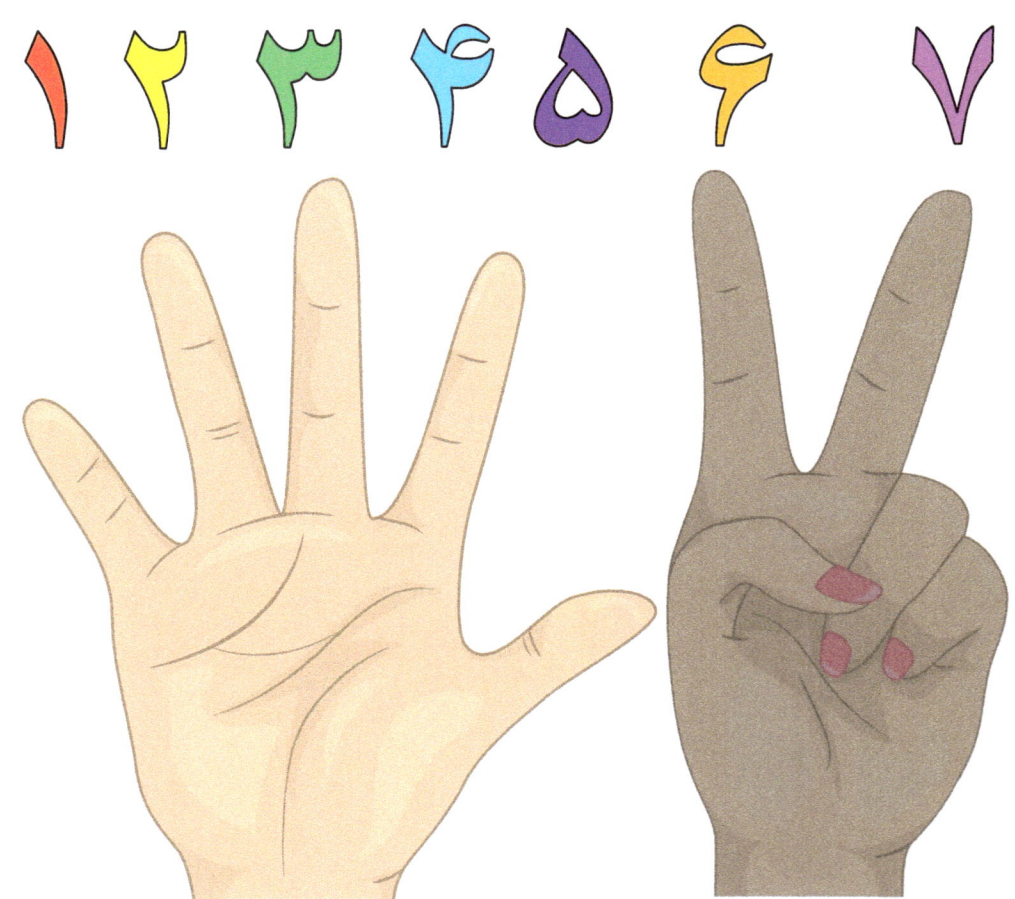

seven

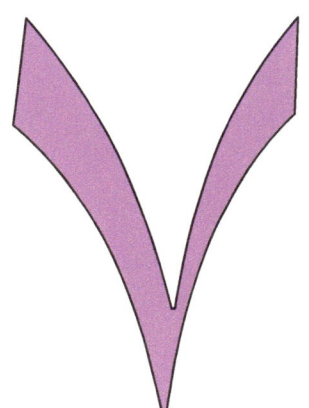

haft

هَفت

۱ ۲ ۳ ۴ ۵ ۶ ۷ ۸

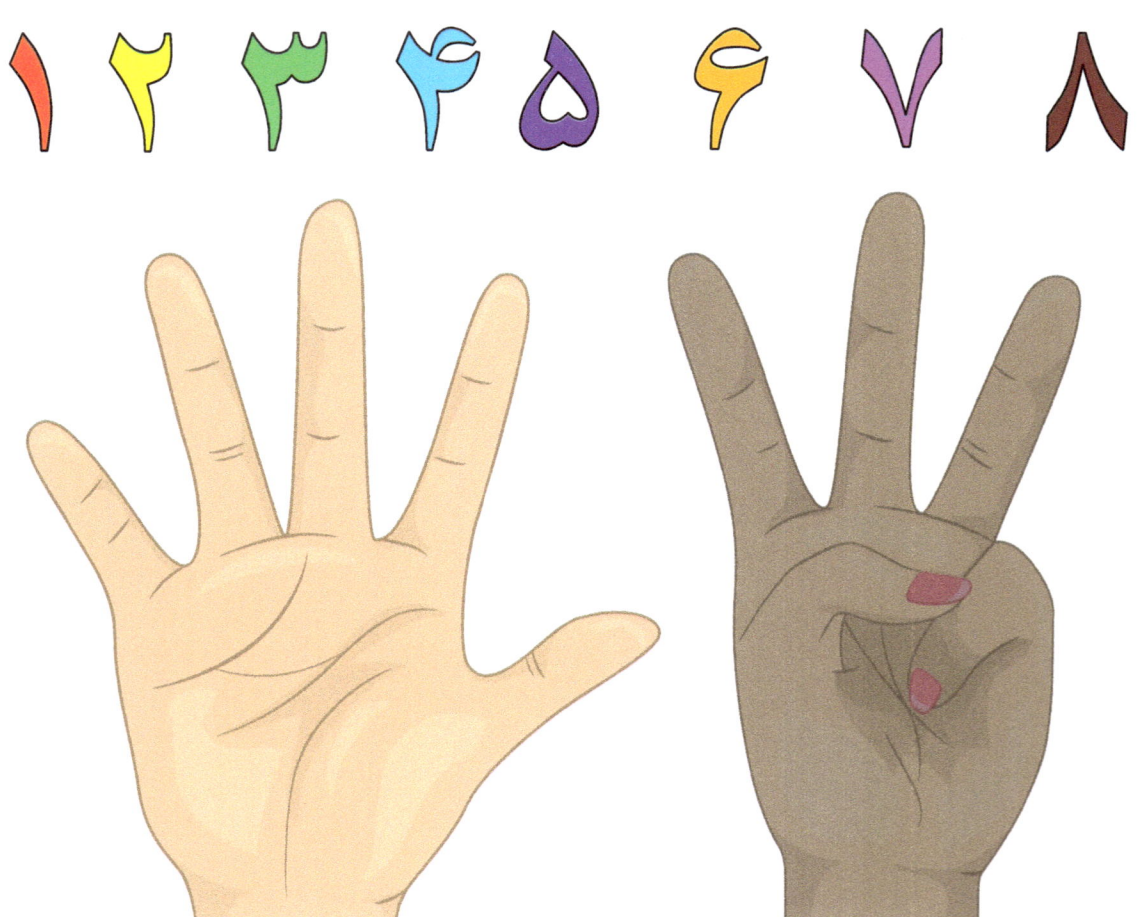

eight

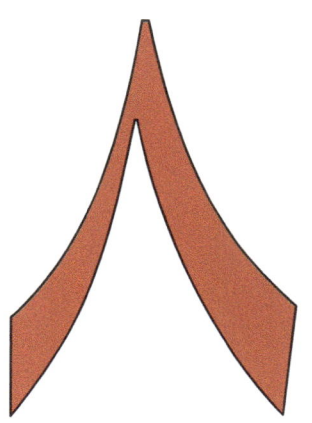

hasht
هَشت

۱ ۲ ۳ ۴ ۵ ۶ ۷ ۸ ۹

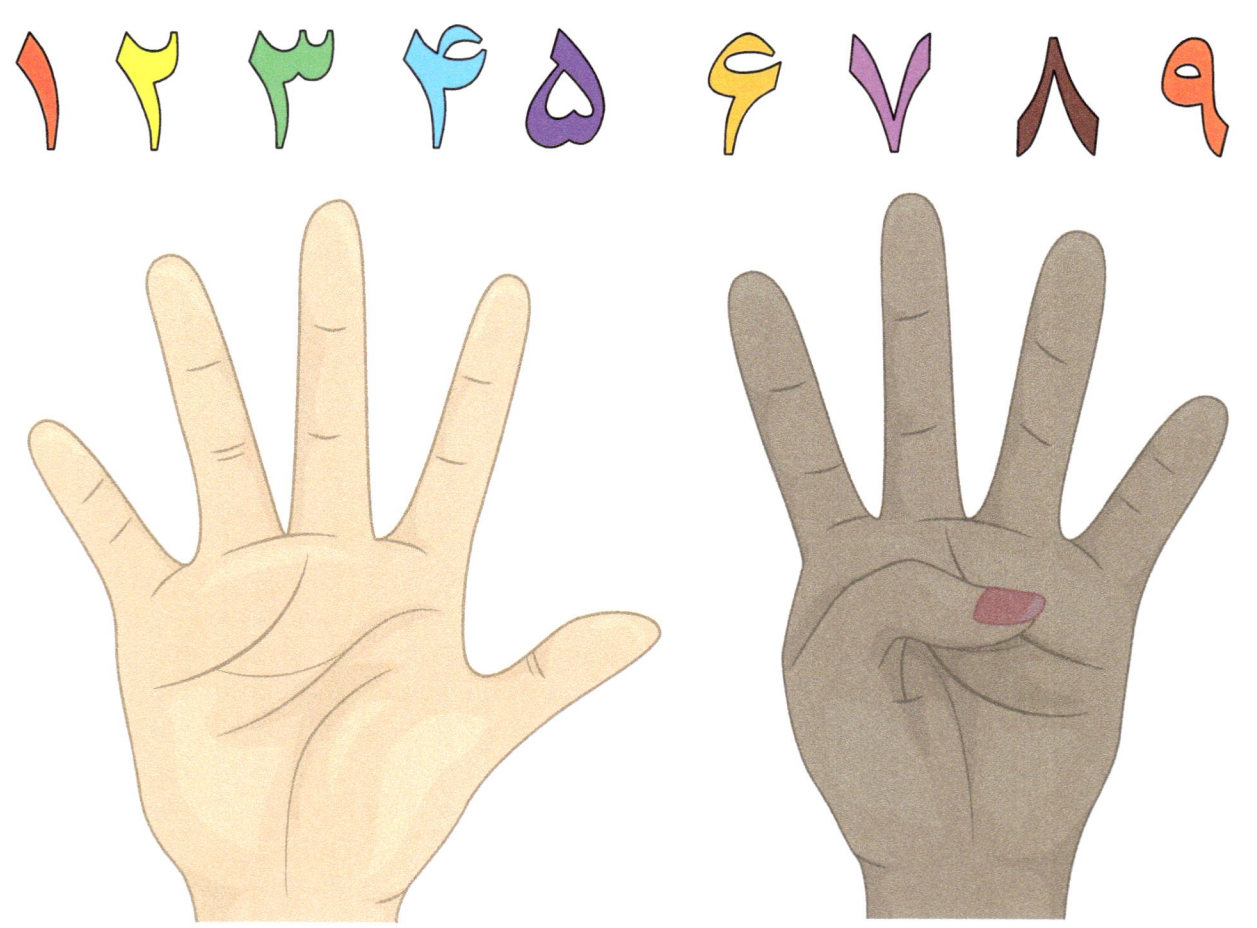

nine

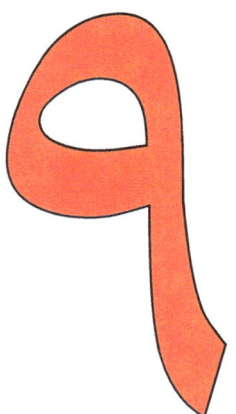

noh
نُه

۱ ۲ ۳ ۴ ۵ ۶ ۷ ۸ ۹ ۰

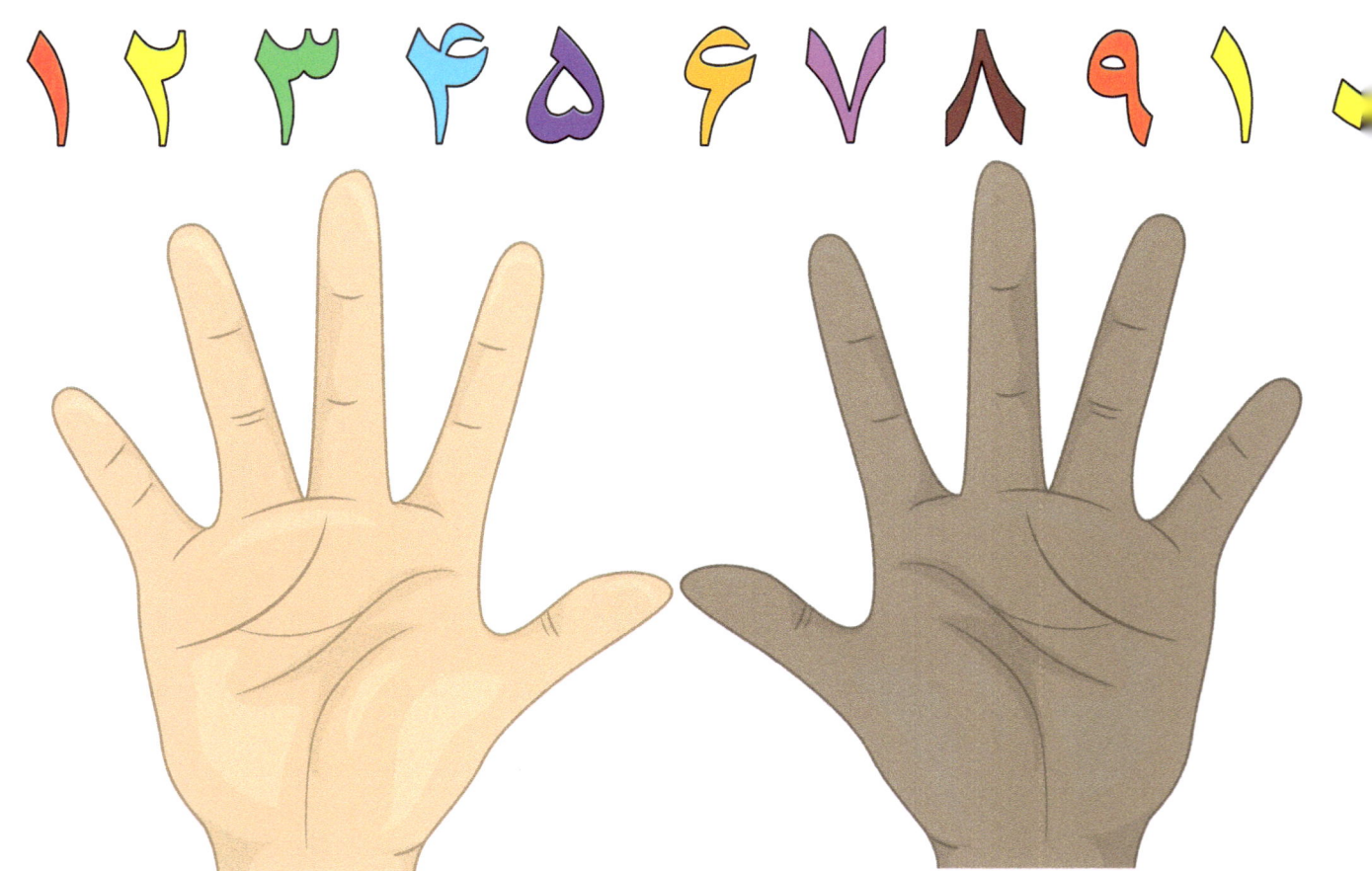

ten

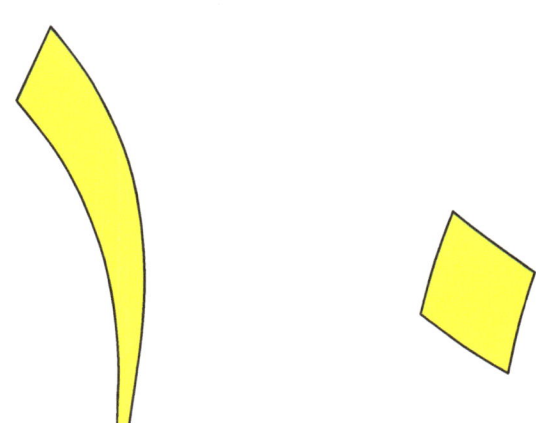

dah

دَه

What is the time?

Sá'at chand ast?
ساعَت چَند اَست؟

á: as (a) in arm

It is 7 [seven] o'clock

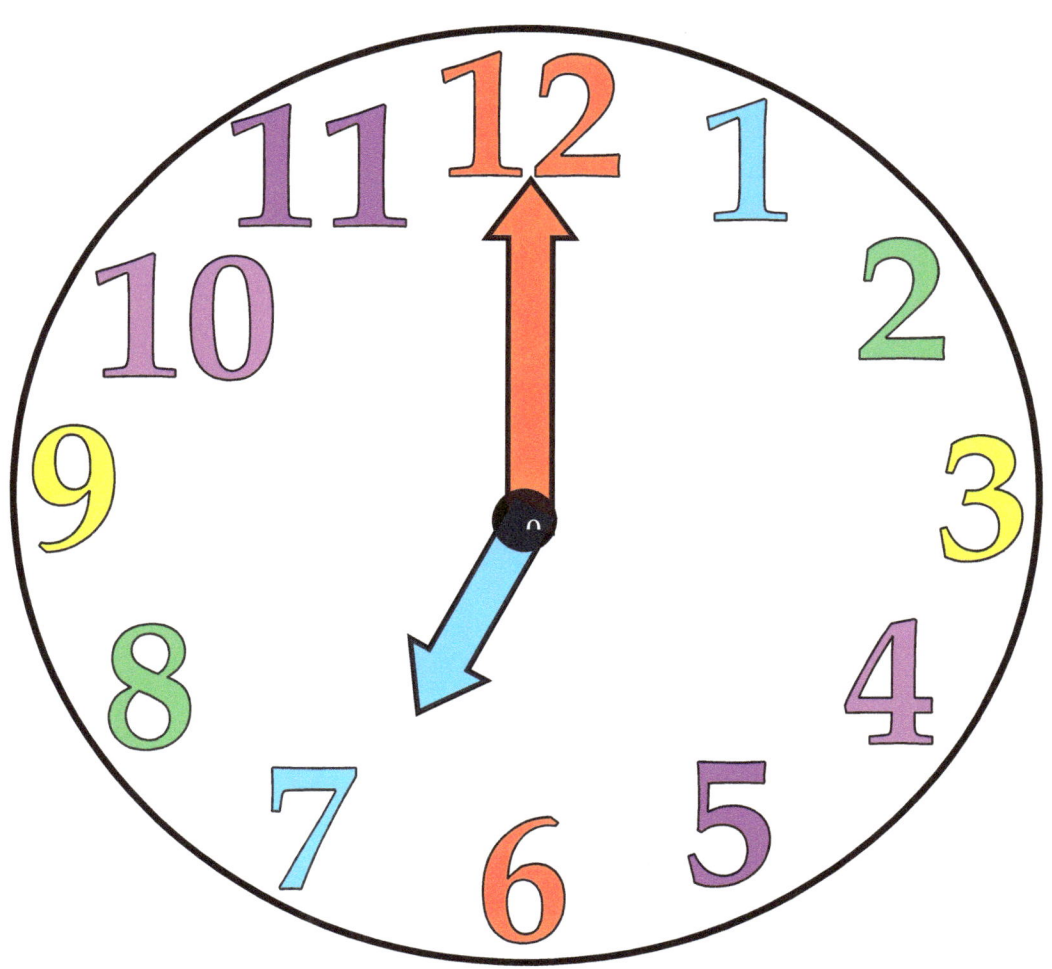

Sá'at ۷ [haft] ast.
ساعَت هَفت اَست

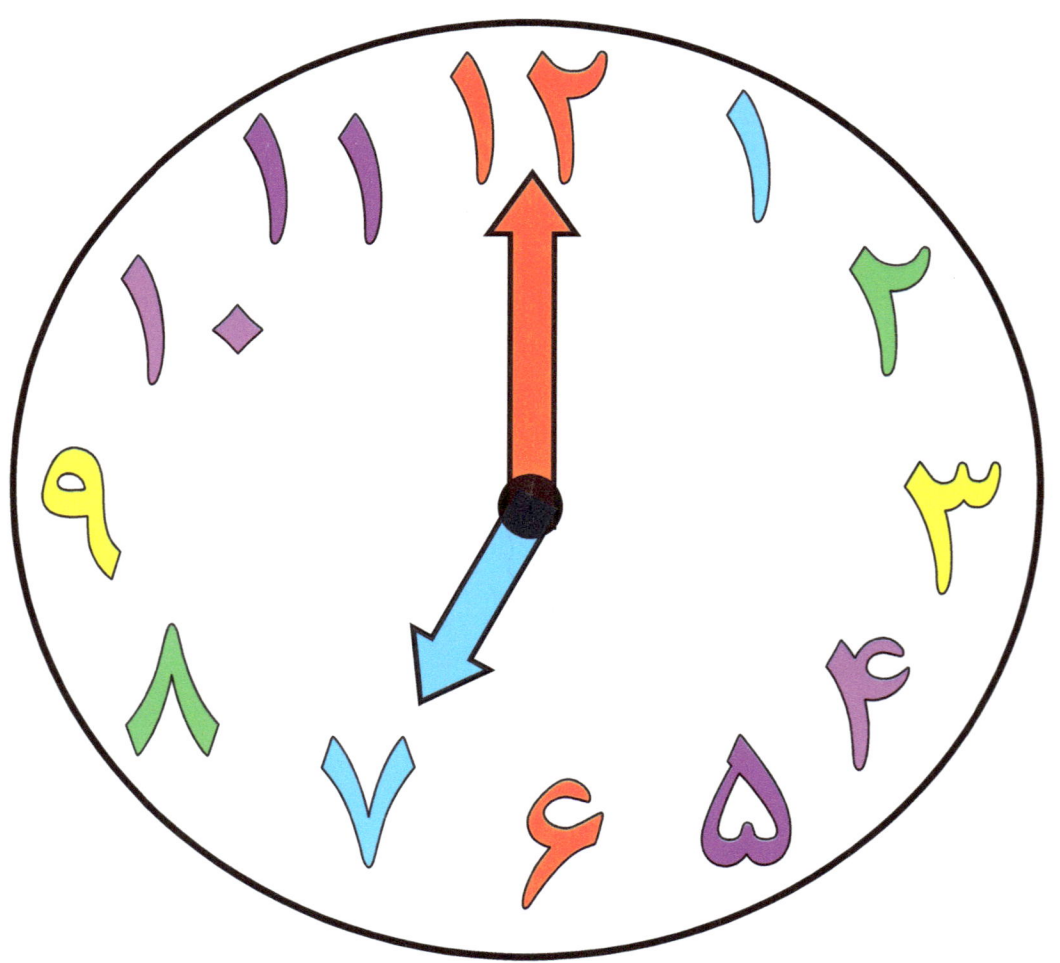

á: as (a) in <u>a</u>rm

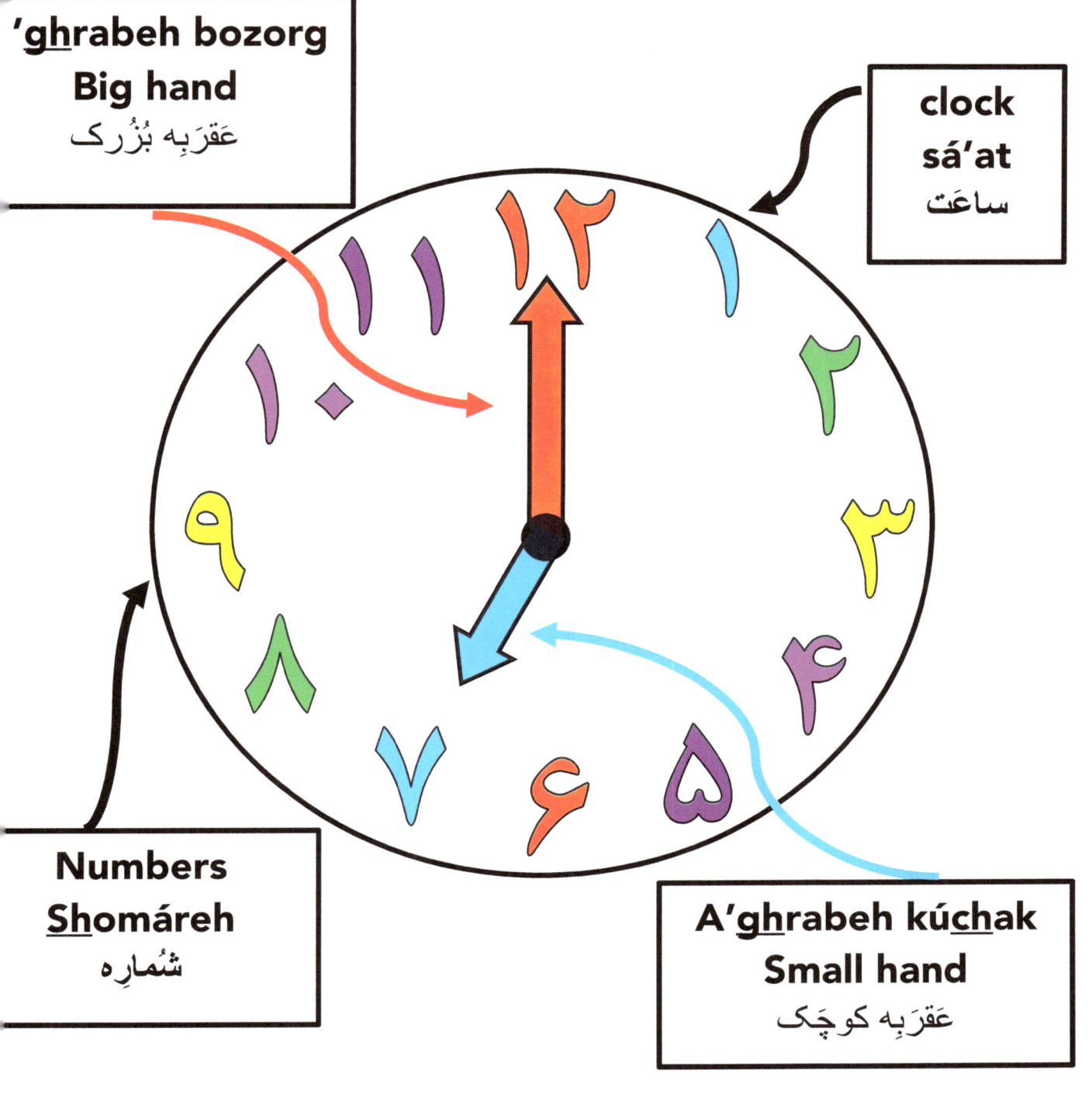

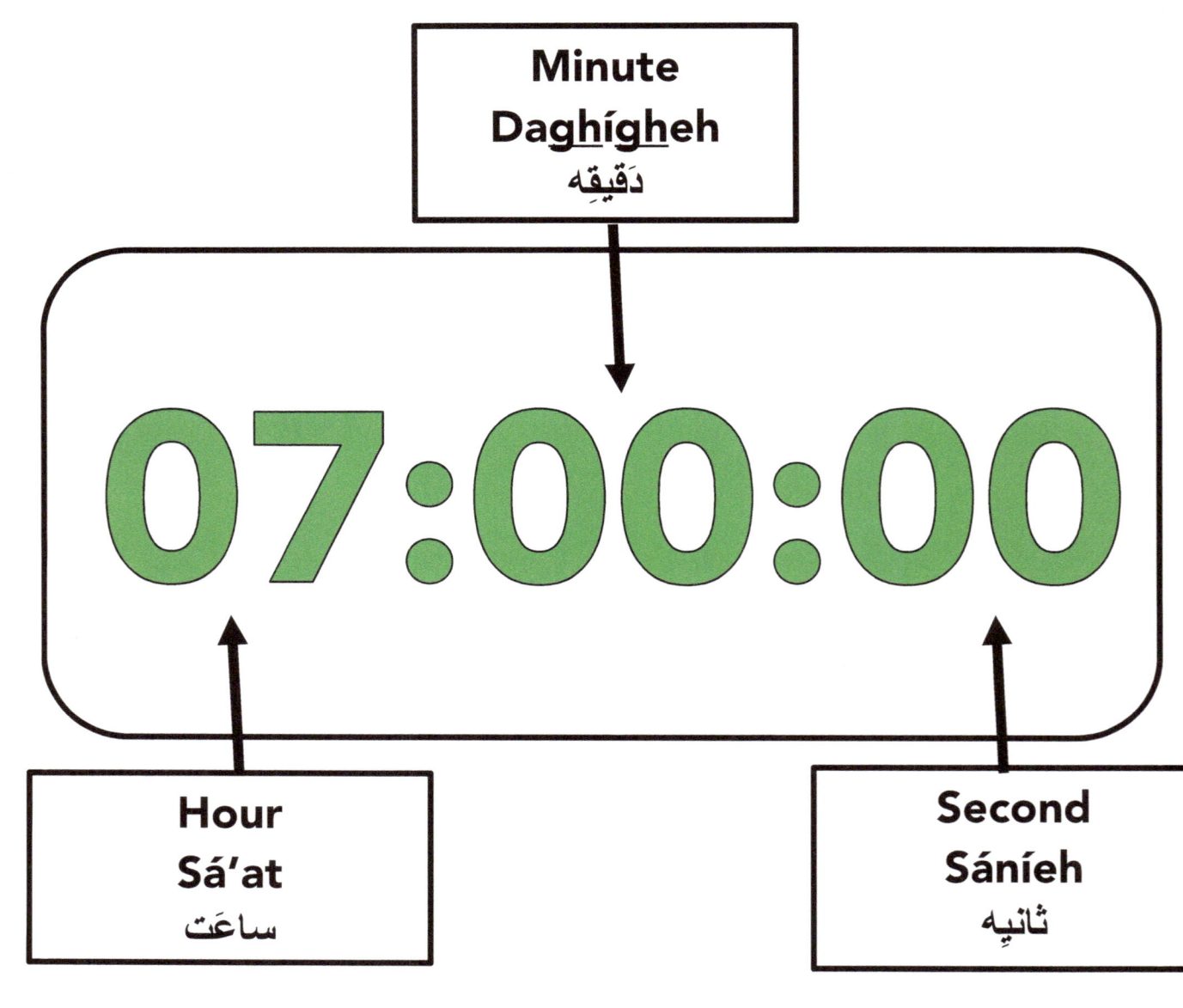

Maths
Ríází
رياضى

í: as (ee) in m<u>ee</u>t
á: as (a) in <u>a</u>rm

plus/addition

jam' kardan
جَمع کردَن
(ezáfeh kardan / ezáfeí)

minus/take away from

menhá

مِنها

(manfí / tafrígh)

á: as (a) in arm
í: as (ee) in meet

divide by

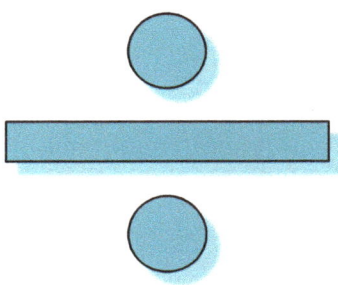

taghsím kardan
تَقسيم کردَن

í: as (ee) in m<u>ee</u>t

multiply by

zarb kardan
ضَرب کردَن

equal

mosáví

مُساوى

(barábar)

á: as (a) in arm
í: as (ee) in meet

weight

vazn

وَزن

Quick Reference: Numbers

English	Finglisi™	Persian
one	yek	یِک
two	do	دو
three	seh	سِه
four	chahár	چَهار
five	panj	پَنج
six	shesh	شِش
seven	haft	هَفت
eight	hasht	هَشت
nine	noh	نُه
ten	dah	دَه
eleven	yázdah	یازدَه
twelve	davázdah	دَوازدَه
thirteen	sízdah	سیزدَه
fourteen	chahárdah	چَهاردَه
fifteen	pánzdah	پانزدَه
sixteen	shánzdah	شانزدَه

Quick Reference: Numbers & Time

English	Finglisi™	Persian
one hundred	yek sad	یِک صَد
one thousand	yek hezár	یِک هزار
second	sáníeh	ثانیه
minute	daghígheh	دَقیقِه
hour	sá'at	ساعَت
clock	sá'ate dívárí	ساعَتِ دیواری
watch	sá'ate mochí	ساعَتِ مُچی
time	vaght	وَقت
numbers	shomáreh	شُماره
watch	sá'at	ساعَت
first	aval[ín]	اَوَلین
second	dovom[ín]	دُومین
third	sevom[ín]	سِومین
fourth	chahárom[ín]	چَهارُمین
fifth	panjom[ín]	پَنجُمین
sixth	sheshom[ín]	شِشُمین
tenth	dahom[ín]	دَهُمین

Quick Reference: Maths

English	Finglisi™	Persian
maths	ríází	ریاضی
to calculate	hesáb kardan	حِساب کردَن
plus/addition	jam' kardan	جَمع کردَن
minus	menhá	مِنها
divide by	taghsím kardan	تَقسیم کردَن
multiply by	zarb kardan	ضَرب کردَن
equal	vaght	مُساوی
weight	vazn	وَزن
English	Englísí	اِنگلیسی
Persian	Fársí	فارسی

www.ingramcontent.com/pod-product-compliance
Lightning Source LLC
Chambersburg PA
CBHW061759290426
44109CB00030B/2897